Explanation of
Calvary in the I

MW00723420

Jesus appears in the cover photograph hanging on the Cross in the ıuclear cloud of a French H-Bomb explosion. Near the Cross to His ight at the edge of the cloud stands His Mother.

"Near the Cross of Jesus there stood His Mother. . . . " (John 19:25).

Abortion centers are the Calvaries of the modern world since here he innocent Christ is re-crucified in the innocent, helpless, unborn hildren. Jesus said, "Whatever you do to the least of my brothers, that ou do unto me." (Matthew 25:45).

Blessed Mother Teresa said, "The fruit of abortion is nuclear war!"

On October 13, 1973, at Akita, Japan, Our Lady said, "If men do not epent and better themselves, the Father will inflict a terrible punish-nent on all humanity. It will be a punishment greater than the deluge, uch as one will never have seen before. Fire will fall from the sky and vill wipe out a great part of humanity, the good as well as the bad, paring neither priests nor faithful. The survivors will find themselves o desolate that they will envy the dead. The only arms which will re-nain for you will be the Rosary and the Sign left by my Son. Each day ecite the prayers of the Rosary. With the Rosary, pray for the Pope, the 3ishops and the priests."

"Pray very much the prayers of the Rosary. I alone am able still to ave you from the calamities which approach. Those who place their onfidence in me will be saved."

Our Lady still appears throughout the world pleading for prayer and asting to bring conversions and peace or to suffer chastisements. She varned Father Gobbi of the Marian Movement of Priests while he was n the United States, "Abortions – these killings of innocent children, hat cry for vengeance before the face of God – have spread and are erformed in every part of this country. The moment of the divine jus-ice and mercy has arrived! You will know the hour of weakness and overty; the hour of suffering and defeat; the purifying hour of the reat chastisements."

Chastisements

How to Prepare

and

Pray Against Them

*A Practical Handbook that explains the
What and Why of Chastisements,
Warnings of Chastisements,
Prayers for Protection Against them,
How to Endure and Survive Them
and Hope for the Future*

DAN LYNCH

JKMI PRESS
ST. ALBANS, VERMONT

ISBN 0-9647988-6-7
Copyright © 2004 Dan Lynch

Contents

Part One:
Jesus King of All Nations' Warning and Devotion

What is the urgent Warning of chastisement from Jesus King of All Nations?

Jesus' "Secretary," a woman mystic, received a message on August 25, 2004 containing an urgent warning of a chastisement soon to come. Jesus' words are in italics, followed by scripture, the living Word of God. Jesus dictated the message and referred His Secretary to the scripture that confirms the message. **Let those who have ears hear!**

Our Lord: *"I command you to write."* "The king then gave the order." (1 Kings 2:46). *"Daughter, I have come to give you a message of grave importance."* "O, that today you would hear his voice: 'Harden not your hearts.' " (Psalm 95:7,8).
"Pray, pray, pray! Prayer offered to Me through My Holy Mother. Only she can avert the chastisement that now swiftly approaches." "Behold, the hour is coming and has arrived." (John 16:32). *"I cry out My little one to all mankind and in particular to My faithful ones! You MUST pray and offer sacrifices! A most fearful punishment is close at hand."* "They shall bear the consequences of their sin." (Ezekiel 44:10).
"Cities will be simultaneously affected. Great destruction, great loss of life. Great sorrow and pain. Smoke and fire. Wailing and lamentation." "Thus says the Lord, Israel's King and redeemer, the Lord of hosts: I am the first and I am the last; there is no God but me. Who is like me? Let him stand up and speak, make it evident, and confront me with it. Who of old announced future events? Let them foretell to us the things to come. Fear not, be not troubled: did I not announce and foretell it long ago? You are my witnesses! Is there a God or any Rock besides me?" (Isaiah 44:6-8).
"My children, I do not wish to strike you in My perfect justice. But if you remain obstinate of heart and blinded by your great pride, I must do so in order to save the greater number." "But now, O our God, what can we say after all this? For we have abandoned your commandments, which you gave through your servants the prophets." (Ezra 9:10,11).
"My child, I tell you most solemnly that this event will take place on a holy day. I, the Lord, have spoken." "Therefore you rebuke offenders little by little, warn them, and remind them of the sins they are committing, that they may abandon their wickedness and believe in you, O Lord!" (Wisdom 12:2).

1

Did Jesus prophesy the Asian Tsunami?

On August 25, 2005, Jesus King of All Nations prophesied a chastisement soon to come. It was Jesus' first public message in 11 years! Jesus said,

> *Pray, pray, pray! Prayer offered to Me through My Holy Mother. Only she can avert the chastisement that now swiftly approaches. I cry out My little one to all mankind and in particular to My faithful ones! You MUST pray and offer sacrifices!* ***A most fearful punishment is close at hand.*** *Cities will be simultaneously affected. Great destruction, great loss of life. Great sorrow and pain. Smoke and fire. Wailing and lamentation.*
>
> *My children, I do not wish to strike you in My perfect justice. But if you remain obstinate of heart and blinded by your great pride, I must do so in order to save the greater number. My child, I tell you most solemnly that this event will take place on a holy day. I, the Lord, have spoken.*
> (For the complete message, with the scriptural confirmations of Jesus, see page 1.)

In my opinion, the Asian Tsunami fulfilled Jesus' prophecy. As Jesus prophesied, the tsunami struck "on a holy day" (Sunday), and cities were "simultaneously affected" with "great destruction, great loss of life" and "smoke and fire" (crematory funeral pyres). Jesus said that this disaster could have been averted, but not enough people prayed and offered sacrifices through His Mother's mediation as He requested.

What did Jesus say after the Asian Tsunami struck on December 26, 2004?

Two days after the Asian Tsunami struck, on December 28, the Feast of the Holy Innocents, Jesus gave another message. He said,

"In the presence of the king" (Esther 1:6)

Our Blessed Lord: *"Daughter of My Sacred Kingship! Cry out; cry out to My children! Repent! Repent and return to the Lord! NEAR IS THE DAY OF THE LORD! A day of swift and perfect justice. Purifying justice.* "Thus says the Lord God: Disaster upon disaster! See it coming! An end is coming, the end is coming upon you! See it coming! The climax has come for you who dwell in the land! The time has come, near is the day: a day of consternation, not of rejoicing. Soon now I will pour out my fury upon you and spend my anger upon you; I will judge you according to your conduct and lay upon you the consequences of all your abominations. .... See, the day of the Lord! See, the end is coming! Lawlessness is in full bloom, insolence flourishes, violence has risen to support wickedness. It shall not be long in coming, nor shall it delay. The time has come, the day dawns." (Ezekiel 7:5-8, 10-11)

My little one, I lament. I weep. "I unceasingly admonished each of you with tears." (Acts 20:31) *My children do not hear. They do not see. They stop their ears that they may not hear. They cover their eyes that they may not see. They are willfully blind and willfully deaf.* "The fear of the Lord is the beginning of knowledge; wisdom and instruction fools despise. .... For the self-will of the simple kills them, the smugness of fools destroys them. But he who obeys me dwells in security, in peace, without fear of harm." (Proverbs 1:7, 1:32-33)

I have shaken the earth to awaken the conscience of man. (Note: On Sunday, December 26, 2004, a most terrible earthquake took place under the Indian Ocean spawning great tidal waves which killed thousands of people, causing great destruction and grieving of hearts. This took place exactly four months and one day after the warning Our Lord gave on August 25, 2004) "The Lord roars from Zion, and from Jerusalem raises his voice; The heavens and the earth quake, but the Lord is a refuge to his people, a stronghold to the men of Israel." (Joel 4:16)

Will they hear? Will they wake from their sleep in sin? "For as it was in the day of Noah, so it will be at the coming of the Son of Man. In those days before the flood, they were eating and drinking, marrying and giving in marriage, up to the day that Noah entered the ark. They did not know until the flood came and carried them all away. So will it be also at the coming of the Son of Man. .... Therefore, stay awake! For you do not know on which day your Lord will come." (Matthew 24:37-39, 42)

If they do not, a yet more terrible catastrophe will befall mankind. Pray! Sacrifice! Invoke My Most Sacred, Eucharistic and Kingly Heart through My Most Holy Mother! "The mother of my Lord" (Luke 1:43)

Child, I have given a GREAT REMEDY in My devotion of Jesus, King of All Nations. I ask My children to embrace this devotion. To pray this devotion. To invoke Me as Jesus, King of All Nations. My Mercy and Protection will cover those souls, families and nations that invoke Me thus. I will stretch forth to them My scepter of Mercy that they may take firm hold and not let go of My Divine Will and Law. I will cover them with My Kingly Mantle that My Perfect Justice may not reach them as it will reach those who have abandoned My Law. "Indeed the Lord will be there with us, majestic; yes, the Lord our judge, the Lord our lawgiver, the our king, he it is who will save us." (Isaiah 33:22)

My children, dear children, do not despair. There is always hope. "Take courage, it is I, do not be afraid! He got into the boat with them and the wind died down." (Mark 6:50-51) *My holy and dear Mother has instructed you many times in many places how to bring down My Mercy upon the world. This Woman of Hope, still pleads for you all, her children.* "Blessed are you daughter, by the Most High God, above all the women on earth; and blessed be the Lord God, the creator of heaven and earth who guided your blow at the head of the chief of our enemies. Your deed of hope will never be forgotten by those who tell of the might of God. May God make this redound to your everlasting honor, rewarding you with blessings, ... you averted our disaster, walking uprightly before our God." (Judith 13:18-20) *Souls underestimate the power of Mary's prayers. One glance from My dear Mother is enough to disarm My Perfect Justice. She is the channel of My Mercy. Through her flows My Life to mankind. Trust your Mother. Honor your Mother. Beseech your Mother to pray for the world. She gathers your prayers and sacrifices and presents them to Me perfumed with the fragrant incense of her love.*

Children, My children, do not despair. "Rejoice in hope, endure in affliction, persevere in prayer." (Romans 12:12) *Come to My Throne of Mercy, confident that I will hear you. I reign in the Most Blessed Sacrament. Adore Me there. Receive Me with hearts full of love and submission to My Holy Will. I need you My faithful ones. Help Me to save souls.* "These alone are my co-workers for the kingdom of God, and they have been a comfort to me." (1 Thessalonians 4:11) *Many are perishing due to obstinate hearts. They must desire salvation, I will not force it upon them for I will not take away their free will. However, My grace and mercy can melt even the most obstinate heart, but you must pray for these graces.* "Just as you once disobeyed God but have now received mercy because of their disobedience, so they have now disobeyed in order that, by virtue of the mercy shown to you, they too may now receive mercy. For God delivered all to disobedience, that he might have mercy upon all." (Romans 11:30-32)

All is coming to fulfillment. Be at peace. Trust in My mercy and love. Pray to My Holy Mother. Entrust your lives to her. Receive the sacraments worthily and frequently. Obey My holy Spouse, the Church. Remain faithful. I love you. I bless you. "For I did not receive it from a human being, nor was I taught it, but it came through a revelation of Jesus Christ." (Galatians 1:12)

Jesus prophesied a Caribbean Tsunami that was averted through the devotional prayers in 1993. The Asian Tsunami could have been averted just like the Caribbean Tsunami but there was an insufficient response of prayer and sacrifice. **You can help to avert Jesus' prophesied "yet more terrible catastrophe"** and future natural disasters like the recent Asian

Tsunami, California mudslides and Eastern blizzard, and the earthquakes, floods, hurricanes and terrorist attacks that we have suffered during the beginning of this Third Millennium. Give Jesus a gift and **Practice the Four Ps: Please** Jesus, **Pray** the devotional prayers, **Promote** the Devotion and **Protect** your family, friends and loved ones. Please distribute our Handbook on Chastisements, call us toll free for discount for bulk quantities for you to distribute to your family, friends, prayer groups and churches.

What did Our Lady say about her Son's Devotion?

Our Lady gave this message to Jesus' Secretary on January 30, 2005:

"This Devotion of Jesus King of all Nations is a treasure house of grace from my Divine Son Jesus. Let all souls embrace this holy Devotion by means of which my Divine Son is honored and souls are brought to conversion." . . . He will turn many of the children of Israel to the Lord their God." (Luke 1:16). *Listen to my Son. Listen, dear children to my beloved Son, your Sovereign Lord and King. DO WHATEVER HE TELLS YOU."* "Indeed, she reaches from end to end mightily and governs all things well." (Wisdom 8:1)

Who is Jesus King of All Nations?

Jesus King of All Nations is a title derived from Sacred Scripture. He is referred to as the ruler of the Kings of the earth (Revelation 1:5), the King of kings and Lord of lords (Revelation 19:6) to whom "all nations shall come and worship in (His) presence" (Revelation 15:4) and who shall judge all nations which will be assembled before Him sitting upon His royal throne. (Matthew 25:31‐32). His kingship is taught in the Encyclical Letter *Quas Primas* by Pope Pius XI.

What is the Jesus King of All Nations Devotion?

Jesus King of All Nations revealed Himself, images, prayers, promises, messages and a devotion to two American women from 1988 to the present. Their revelations confirmed one another. In humility they wish to remain anonymous. The Devotion to Him is the Jesus King of All Nations Devotion. (See www.JKMI.com).

Is the Devotion approved by the Church?

The Devotion is consistent with scripture, Tradition and the Teaching

Authority of the Church. *The Journal* of the Devotion has been granted the *Nihil Obstat* that is a declaration by the Church that it is free of doctrinal and moral error.

Bishop Enrique Hernandez Rivera, D.D. of Caguas, Puerto Rico said that he "recognized the need to foster more devotion to Our Lord and Savior Jesus Christ, True King of All Nations." He wished us "all the best in your efforts of spreading the message of Christ to all who invoke Him by this title." Some of the revelations of this Devotion occurred in Puerto Rico.

What did Jesus King of All Nations say about His Devotion?

Jesus said, *"I have come to entrust to you a message of great importance for the world. I tell you . . . the days are coming when Mankind will cry out to Me for mercy. I tell you, My child, only one thing will be given as a remedy. I Myself AM that remedy! Let souls give devotion to Me through My Most Holy Mother, who mediates to Me on their behalf, as 'Jesus King of All Nations.' "*

Is the Devotion like the Divine Mercy and Sacred Heart Devotions?

Jesus said, *"This devotion to Me as 'Jesus King of All Nations' is to be a companion devotion to that of My Mercy as given to My beloved daughter, Faustina, and to that of My Sacred Heart as given to My beloved daughter, Margaret Mary."*

What are the elements of the Devotion?

The Devotion consists of images of Jesus King of All Nations and Jesus our Eucharistic King with St. Michael the Archangel, a medal bearing their images, and prayers and promises. The prayers are the Chaplet of Unity, the Novena of Chaplets, the Novena in honor of Jesus as True King, the Novena of Holy Communions, the Litany in honor of Jesus King of All Nations, the Consecration to Mary, Mediatrix of All Grace and the Special Blessing.

What are the promises of the Devotion?

The promises to those who embrace this Devotion are the graces of conversion, healing, final perseverance, unity, peace in hearts and homes, a special grace emanating from the Sacred and Immaculate Hearts, the gifts of the Holy Spirit, protection from harm and mitigation of chastisements and all forms of God's justice. Jesus said, ***"tremendous* will be the mira-**

6

cles of grace that I will work through this image and Devotion of Mine."
Why did Jesus give us this Devotion?

Jesus gave us this Devotion out of love for us because He wants to reign in mercy in all hearts so that His reign will recognized on earth and there will be unity in one flock and one shepherd. He wants the proclamation of the dogma of Mary as Mediatrix of All Grace. He wants to grant us graces of forgiveness, conversion, healing, protection and peace.

How is the Devotion practiced?

The Devotion is practiced by embracing and living the Word of sacred scripture, by the wearing of the medal, veneration of the Image, the recitation of the prayers, adoration of the Blessed Sacrament and the reception of the sacraments of Penance and the Eucharist.

A large Visitation Image of Jesus King of All Nations has journeyed throughout the world, receiving the veneration of thousands. Many signs, wonders, healings and conversions have been reported. The Image is sent to local Guardian Teams who have requested Visitations. They prepare the reception and coordinate all liturgical events with the local pastors. The Visitations often include churches, monasteries, convents, prisons, hospitals, abortion centers, nursing homes and schools. Please contact us if you would like to host a Visitation.

What is the end goal of the Devotion?

Jesus said, *"My child, I would have My faithful ones know that the end goal of this Devotion and indeed of all devotions, is that of true love and worship of me, their God and the sanctification and resulting salvation of their souls."*

He also said, ***"I want to reign in __all__ hearts!!!*** *My throne on this earth remains in the hearts of __all__ men. I most particularly reign in the Most Holy Eucharist, and in loving hearts that believe in Me, that speak with Me, and I tell you, My daughter, that I do speak in the hearts of all men."*

How will Jesus reign in all hearts?

The reign of Jesus is established in our hearts by our consecration and reparation to His Sacred Heart. Pope Pius XII said, "It demands the full and absolute determination of surrendering an consecrating oneself to the love of the Divine Redeemer. The wounded heart of the Savior (author's note: as seen in the image of Jesus King) is the living sign and symbol of that love. It is likewise clear even to a greater degree, that this devotion especially declares that we must repay divine love with our own love."

(Pope Pius XII, Encyclical Letter, *Haurietis Aquas*).

Jesus promised that He *"shall unite all mankind, even unto the end of time, under My divine reign of Kingship. The Merciful reign of My Kingship will be proclaimed everywhere among the nations through which shall come the end - time salvation of mankind by Unity in My Holy Catholic Church."*

In His mercy, Jesus gives us an opportunity to recognize His reign now before He reclaims it in His Justice. We should accept this opportunity and "approach the throne of grace and receive mercy." (Hebrews 4:16).

What prayers can we say that will recognize Christ's kingship?

Jesus told His "Secretary", the mystic of the Devotion, *"Mankind **must** recognize my Divine Kingship, my Divine Rights over them! It is only in Me, my child, that mankind will find peace."* (*The Journal of the Devotion* 160).

We can recognize His Divine Kingship, as Jesus requested, by praying the Novena in Honor of Jesus as True King. Jesus told His "Secretary," *"These prayers are most efficacious when prayed before My image."* (*The Journal of the Devotion* 29).

Pope Pius XI said, "When once men recognize, both in private and in public life, that Christ is King, society will at last receive the great blessings of real liberty, well-ordered discipline, peace and harmony." (Encyclical Letter *Quas Primas)*. That's why Jesus King revealed to us the ejaculation, *"O Jesus King of All Nations, may your reign be recognized on earth."*

Can you explain the elements of the image of Jesus King of All Nations shown on the inside of the front cover?

The image of Jesus shows him as King of All Nations crowned and holding a scepter of mercy in His right hand. Above the scepter are three concentric rings as in an atom, which symbolizes unity in God in the Holy Trinity, in His Church, and in nations. The small particle in the atom symbolizes the Church and Our Lady, both espoused to God. Rays of light shine from His wounds that symbolize His merciful graces. Blood flows from his wounded Sacred Heart upon all nations, which symbolizes His Love.

Jesus said, *"This image is a sign that I rule Heaven and earth, and My Kingdom, My Reign, is near at hand...Give this image to mankind as a source of graces and of peace. **My Most Holy Mother is preparing the Great Triumph. The Triumph of Her Immaculate Heart ushers in the Reign of My Love and Mercy. This image, my child, must become known. Tremendous will be the miracles of grace that I will work through this image an Devotion of Mine."***

"Great are the graces which will be granted through the proper venera-tion of this Image of Mine." (*The Journal of the Devotion* 6).

Can you explain the elements of the image of St. Michael the Archangel shown on the inside of the back cover?

The image of St. Michael shows him next to the Sacred Host from which drops of the Precious Blood drip into a chalice below. St. Michael the Archangel appeared to Jesus' Secretary. She said, "I saw him gaze up to heaven at the God he so loves and defends, with reverence and a tremendous look that denoted great love and an overpowering sense of awe. When I think of St. Michael's face, I remember the tremendous power and majesty of this holy archangel, but also of the gentle kindness with which he looked at me." (*The Journal of the Devotion* 87).

St. Michael spoke, *"I am the Archangel Michael. I have come to you to proclaim news of great importance. I hold out to you the image of a like-ness of me. My friend, it is the most holy will of God that a medal be made in particular honor of me as the Protector of His Church on earth."* (*The Journal of the Devotion* 79, 84-85). This medal was made, as St. Michael requested, with Jesus King of All Nations on the front side and St. Michael on the reverse.

We see St. Michael in flight enveloped in glory with a fiery sword in his right hand raised above his head. His left hand holds a pair of scales over the earth representing God's justice. (Wisdom 1:15). St. Michael wears a crown with sparkling diamonds and surmounted in the front by a cross. To the right of St. Michael above his head appears the Sacred Host with the letters "IHS" and a small cross above them. "IHS" is the monogram de-rived from the Greek word for Jesus. Drops of His Most Precious Blood drip from the Sacred Host into a chalice below.

It was revealed to Jesus' Secretary that around the border should appear the words, "At that time there shall arise Michael, the Great Prince, Guard-ian of Your People." (Daniel 12:1).

St. Michael revealed that God willed that he be honored as "The Protec-tor of the Church of Christ on Earth."

What is the Mission of the Jesus King of All Nations apostolate?

The essential mission of the apostolate of the Jesus King of All Nations Devotion is to bring the recognition of the reign of Jesus King of All Na-tions to earth. This is accomplished by His reign in all hearts through the Consecration to Mary Mediatrix of All Grace, which will result in the unity of all mankind with "one flock, and one Shepherd." (See John 10:16).

The apostolate carries out its mission by promotion of the Devotion's images, medal, prayers and promises. The images are of Jesus King of All Nations; Jesus Our Eucharistic King with St. Michael the Archangel, Protector of the Blessed Sacrament; and Jesus Christ Mediator, Our Lady Mediatrix of All Grace. The medal contains the first two of these images with ejaculatory prayers. The prayers are The Chaplet of Unity, The Novena of Communions, The Novena in Honor of Jesus as True King, The Litany in Honor of Jesus King of All Nations, The Special Blessing and The Consecration to Mary, Mediatrix of All Grace.

The apostolate produces and distributes images, medals, books, audio and video tapes and clothing. It coordinates Visitations to parishes and prayer groups of a 4' X 6' Visitation Image of Jesus King of All Nations and Visitations to homes of a smaller Home Image.

All of this is done in union with the Holy Father and in obedience to the Teaching Authority of the Church fortified by prayer, fasting and the sacraments.

What does Jesus King of All Nations promise to those who embrace the Devotion?

Jesus King of All Nations promises to those who embrace the Devotion graces of healings, conversions, forgiveness, protection, final perseverance, peace in hearts and homes, a special power with the Sacred and Immaculate Hearts, the gifts of the Holy Spirit and mitigation of the severity of chastisements.

Who is Jesus' Secretary?

Jesus' Secretary is a humble, married American woman. She is one of the women who receives the revelations of Jesus King of All Nations. Jesus called her His "Secretary" because she acts as such in receiving and transcribing His messages, similar to a secretary who takes dictation in a business office. That is her job description.

However, Jesus also calls her "my daughter," "my child," and "my little one," because that is her relation to Him.

How was the August 25, 2004 urgent Warning received?

Jesus dictated His Warning to His Secretary and referred her to scripture. She transcribed the dictation and read and wrote down the scripture. The scripture, which is the living Word of God, confirms the dictated message.

Part Two
Warnings and Chastisements

What is a warning from Jesus?

A "warning" is a call to change, to conversion and repentance from sin to grace or to suffer from a chastisement or punishment. A father warns his teenage child, "If you don't stop using drugs, you can't use the car!" Similarly, the prophets warned us to stop sinning or be punished. God never inflicts chastisements without warning us through His servants, the prophets. God's love for His sinful children is shown through the prophets who issue warnings to turn back to God and pray and fast or to suffer chastisements.

Did Jesus ever give a warning in the Bible?

Jesus gave the same warning that the prophet John the Baptist gave, "Repent! (Change your ways!) The Kingdom of Heaven is near." (Matthew 4:17). After the Tower of Siloam killed some people, Jesus was asked if they were more guilty than all of the others in Jerusalem. He replied, "Certainly not! But I tell you, unless you repent, you will all perish as they did." (Luke 13:5).

Has Jesus King made any other warnings?

Yes. He said, *"My daughter, the world is in grave danger of provoking the wrath of God."* "For great is the day of the Lord, and exceedingly terrible; who can bear it? Yet even now, says the Lord, return to me with your whole heart, with fasting, and weeping, and mourning; Rend your hearts, not your garments, and return to the Lord, your God. For gracious and merciful is He, slow to anger, rich in kindness, and relenting in punishment. Perhaps He will again relent and leave behind Him a blessing. Offerings and libations for the Lord your God." (Joel 2:11-14). (*The Journal of the Devotion* 303).

What is a chastisement ?

A chastisement (also called a punishment or judgment) is a punishment sent by God or by others, and allowed by God, in order to help sinners to convert.

Are there any examples of chastisements in the Bible?

There are many examples of chastisements in the Bible: the Great Flood (Genesis 6:5); the destruction of Sodom and Gomorrah (Genesis 28: 20); the earthquake that swallowed up Core and his followers (Numbers 16: 30); the plagues of Egypt (Exodus 6:6; 12:12) and the evil that came upon other oppressors of Israel (Ezekiel 25: 11; 28: 22); the Babylonian Captivity and the destructions of Jerusalem.

Were there any warnings for any of these biblical chastisements?

Yes. Isaiah, Jeremiah, Ezekiel and Jesus all prophesied the destruction of Jerusalem for its sins. (See Isaiah 1; Jeremiah 1; Ezekiel 23 and Luke 21:5-6; 20-24). These were prophecies of divine chastisements that were fulfilled.

For example, Ezekiel prophesied a terrible chastisement, "For thus says the Lord God: 'Bring up a host against them, and make them an object of terror and a spoil. And the host shall stone them and dispatch them with their swords; they shall slay their sons and their daughters, and burn up their houses. Thus will I put an end to lewdness in the land, that all women may take warning and not commit lewdness as you have done. And your lewdness shall be requited upon you, and you shall bear the penalty for your sinful idolatry; and you shall know that I am the Lord God.' " (Ezekiel 23:46-48).

The prophecy was fulfilled and God allowed the destruction of Jerusalem. But He saved a faithful remnant and had them marked by a seal on their forehead. "And the Lord said to him, 'Go through the city, through Jerusalem, and put a mark upon the foreheads of the men who sigh and groan over all the abominations that are committed in it.' And to the others He said in my hearing, 'Pass through the city after him, and smite; your eye shall not spare, and you shall show no pity; slay old men outright, young men and maidens, little children and women, but touch no one upon whom is the mark. And begin at my sanctuary.' So they began with the elders who were before the house. Then He said to them, 'Defile the house, and fill the courts with the slain. Go forth.' So they went forth, and smote in the city. And while they were smiting, and I was left alone, I fell upon my face, and cried, 'Ah Lord God! wilt thou destroy all that remains of Israel in the outpouring of thy wrath upon Jerusalem?' " (Ezekiel 9:4-8).

Jesus also made a future prophecy of the destruction of Jerusalem that was fulfilled with the deaths of tens of thousands by the Roman General Titus in the year 70 A. D. This too was a prophecy of a divine chastisement that was fulfilled. (See Luke 21:5-6; 20-24).

What is God's purpose for chastisements?

God's purpose for chastisements is medicinal – to cure humanity from sin and bring them to repentance and conversion to live in His love and grace. Scripture says that God chastises those He loves. "Whoever is dear to me I reprove and chastise. Be earnest about it, therefore. Repent!" (Revelation 3:19).

The Letter to the Hebrews says that chastisements are to make the righteous holy, just as an earthly father disciplines his sons to help them to be good.

> "My son, do not disdain the discipline of the Lord or lose heart when reproved by Him; for whom the Lord loves, He disciplines; He scourges every son He acknowledges."

> Endure your trials as "discipline;" God treats you as sons. For what "son" is there whom his father does not discipline? If you are without discipline, in which all have shared, you are not sons but bastards.

> Besides this, we have had our earthly fathers to discipline us, and we respected them. Should we not (then) submit all the more to the Father of spirits and live?

> They disciplined us for a short time as seemed right to them, but He does so for our benefit, in order that we may share His holiness. At the time, all discipline seems a cause not for joy but for pain, yet later it brings the peaceful fruit of righteousness to those who are trained by it.

> So strengthen your drooping hands and your weak knees. Make straight paths for your feet, that what is lame may not be dislocated but healed.
>
> (Hebrews 12:5-13).

God does judge. Hell is eternal punishment for unrepented sin. It is a real evil consequent upon wrongdoing and deservedly suffered. But to save us from hell, God chooses to impose chastisements. These are medicinal, intended to discourage us from self-injury by wrongdoing and to encourage us to rectify our lives. Sin is separation from God and violation of His loving plan. Punishment shows sinners what they are doing to themselves. So God permits humankind to experience the consequences of sin. God's chastisements are not for destruction but for *re-construction* – to bring us to repentance and conversion and back to Him and His divine mercy through the forgiveness of our sins. Divine judgments are not to consume us but to purify us. They are not to condemn us but to redeem us. They are not an end but a chance for a new beginning. We can bring this new beginning through prayer (especially the Rosary, the Chaplets of Unity and Mercy and the Novena in Honor of Jesus as True King), fasting and the sacraments of Confession and Communion.

Why does God punish us with chastisements?

God creates everything good, evil comes from creatures' abuse of their freedom, and punishment for sin is not arbitrarily imposed by God. Human punishment often has the character of a more or less vengeful reaction, but God's punishment has nothing of this character.

Without excluding created freedom, God "desires all men to be saved and to come to the knowledge of the truth." (1 Timothy 2-4). Jesus comes to save, not to condemn. (See John 3.17; 12.47).

God's justice ultimately consists in being faithful to His gifts of life and freedom, and God simply cannot be unfaithful. (See 2 Timothy 2.12-13). God tries every means to win the love of sinners who initially reject Him but still might repent. In our Lord Jesus we see how far He goes. "God so loved the world that He gave His only Son." (John 3.16).

What is the predominant sin that causes chastisements?

Abraham Lincoln and Jesus King both said that it was pride. Lincoln said, "Intoxicated with unbroken success, we have become too self-sufficient to feel the necessity of redeeming and preserving grace, too proud to pray to the God that made us."

Jesus King said, *"Your pride blinds you to your God. Pride blinds! They think they see and know the truth, but what they perceive is smoke, it is all falsehood."* (*The Journal of the Devotion* 266).

In His urgent Warning, Jesus King said, *"My children, I do not wish to strike you in My perfect justice. But if you remain obstinate of heart and blinded by your great pride, I must do so in order to save the greater number."*

Does the Bible say that God chastises the innocent?

Yes. In the Letter to the Hebrews it says, "My son, do not regard lightly the discipline of the Lord, nor lose courage when you are punished by Him. For the Lord disciplines him whom He loves, and chastises every son whom He receives." (Hebrews 12:5-6).

Who is a biblical example of an innocent man who suffered chastisements?

Job. God allowed the chastisements of innocent Job for His greater glory. Job's story is told in the Book of Job. He was an innocent man who was "blameless and upright who feared God and avoided evil." (Job 1:1). He had many children and animals and much property and was "greater than any of the men of the East." (Job 1:3). God allowed that he suffer chastisements and lose it all.

How was Job chastised?

The Book of Job shows that God allowed him to be chastised through Satan by means that still happen today – enemy raiders (like today's terrorists), forces of nature such as lightning and great wind (like today's hurricanes or tornados), a loathsome disease causing boils and scabs (like today's AIDS) and the death and loss of property, animals, employees and children.

How is Job a model of a good attitude towards chastisements of innocent people?

Job was humble and realized that God allows the chastisements of innocent people like himself. He recognized that God does not have to justify His actions to men, that He is almighty and omnipotent and that we must humbly accept our suffering and trust in God that "all things work for good for those who love God." (Romans 8:28).

We should say with Job, "Happy is the man whom God reproves! The Almighty's chastening do not reject. For He wounds, but He binds up; He smites, but His hands give healing." (Job 5:17-18).

We should imitate him and also his attitude of resignation to chastisements. Job said, "Naked I came forth from my mother's womb, and naked shall I go back again. The Lord gave and the Lord has taken away; blessed be the name of the Lord!" (Job 1:21) "We accept good things from God; and should we not accept evil?" (Job 2:10).

Finally, we should stop questioning God and trust in His ways of Divine Providence. Job said, "I know that you can do all things and that no purpose of yours can be hindered. I have dealt with great things that I do not understand; things too wonderful for me, which I cannot know. I had heard of you by word of mouth, but now my eye has seen you. Therefore, I disown what I have said, and repent in dust and ashes." (Job 42:2-6).

Who was the totally innocent one that suffered from chastisement?

Jesus Christ, as prophesied by the prophet Isaiah who said, "But He was wounded for our transgressions, He was bruised for our iniquities; upon Him was the chastisement that made us whole, and with His stripes we were healed. . . . But the Lord laid upon Him the guilt of us all." (Isaiah 53:5-6).

Why does God allow the innocent to suffer from chastisements?

God's chastisements can be brought to us through Himself directly (such as the destruction of Sodom and Gomorrah) or through nature (such as the Great Flood) or through the evil hands of others (the Romans' destruction of Jerusalem) resulting in the death of innocent people. Jesus Himself is the prime example. God allows this for a greater good. God's chastisements brings suffering which is mysteriously meritorious to those who accept it, abandon themselves and offer it to Him. Suffering brings us to repentance that brings God's merciful forgiveness, healing and union with Him.

Jesus, who was totally innocent, experienced the consequences of sin and death. He redeemed us from them by His suffering and death. Jesus knew punishment, not because He had sinned, but because He suffered sin's consequences and reconciled humankind with God, restoring the harmony sin had destroyed. (See Isaiah 53:4-12; Matthew 20:28; Colossians 1:19-20; 2:14; Hebrews 9:24-28; 1 Peter 2:24). He reconciled us to Himself and He was the means of expiation through His blood for the eternal punishment of hell that was due to us because of sin. (See 2 Corinthians 5:19; Romans 3:25-26).

Isaiah, Jeremiah and Jesus prophesied the destructions of Jerusalem because of its sins. (See Isaiah 1; Jeremiah 1; Luke 21:5-6; 20-24). These were prophecies of divine chastisements that were fulfilled. Many innocent people were killed in these destructions.

Does God really love us if He allows the innocent to suffer chastisements?

Yes. The Bible assures us that God really loves us. Saint John the Evangelist assures us, "For God so loved the world that He gave His only Son, that whoever believes in Him should not perish but have eternal life. For God sent the Son into the world, not to condemn the world, but that the world might be saved through Him." (John 3:16-17).

God passed before Moses and proclaimed, "The Lord, the Lord, a God merciful and gracious, slow to anger, and abounding in steadfast love and faithfulness, keeping steadfast love for thousands, forgiving iniquity and transgression and sin, but who will by no means clear the guilty, visiting the iniquity of the fathers upon the children and the children's children, to the third and the fourth generation." (Exodus 34:6-7).

Saint John says, "In this the love of God was made manifest among us, that God sent His only Son into the world, so that we might live through Him. In this is love, not that we loved God but that He loved us and sent His Son to be the expiation for our sins. . . .

"So we know and believe the love God has for us. God is love, and he who abides in love abides in God, and God abides in him. In this is love perfected with us, that we may have confidence for the day of judgment, because as He is so are we in this world. There is no fear in love, but perfect love casts out fear. For fear has to do with punishment, and he who fears is not perfected in love." (1 John 9-10; 16-18).

What did Jesus King say about His love for us?

"My little one, please let all my children know how dearly their God loves them. To each soul I say: Believe Me, I love you with an everlasting Love. Look there! (Jesus points to a crucifix in the my room.) Look there and see how much I Love you!" (*The Journal of the Devotion* 257).

"My little one, your Jesus comes to you to let gush forth from the Reservoir that is His Most Sacred Heart, His Infinite Love for all of mankind through these messages of teaching, of LOVE, and of consolation. This, My daughter, this is the Place that I want souls to enter into. My dear little one, tell souls that their God Loves them dearly. I invite all souls into the Ark that is My Most Sacred Heart. Herein, you shall find shelter when the floods of My Justice wash over the earth." (*The Journal of the Devotion* 270 - 271).

"Please! Please, children of men! Hear your God! Your indifferences and outright denial of Me pierces My Heart over and over again! I LOVE you! Oh I love you! So tenderly. So tenderly. I give you My very Heart! I have given you My very Life. I have given you My every drop of blood. I have given you My sweetest and dearest Mother to be your own! Little one, children! The Mother of God is your Mother! Hear her. Oh children of men. How long I have put up with you, because of the Love I bear you. Do you still, still insist on tempting your God to desire that He had not created you? Ah, and yet My children, I still, still LOVE you in spite of yourselves." (*The Journal of the Devotion* 276).

"I offer to each of one of you My Divine and Human Heart to be your Life and your Joy. Your resting place now and in eternity." (*The Journal of Devotion* 297).

Has Jesus King of All Nations given any warnings of chastisements in addition to the August 25, 2004 urgent Warning?

Yes, Jesus said, *"I Am King of Heaven and Earth! ... Hear me, O peoples of the earth! My Reign is near at hand. Turn from your perverse and evil ways! I tell you, unless you turn back to me and repent, I will strike you in My Most Perfect Justice.* Children of men, your God loves you! Why must you be so hard of heart, so as not to reflect upon yourselves and hear the anguished cry of your God?

"My children, your God appeals to you. Now is the time of Great Mercy!!! Take heed and benefit from it. If you do not, a most grievous chastisement will suddenly fall upon you. ... (The Journal of the Devotion 22-23).

"Great is My Love for all mankind. Mankind must heed the warnings I have given and, in particular, those given through My Most Holy mother when in My great mercy I have sent her to her children on earth.

"Mankind must recognize my Divine Kingship, My Divine Rights over them! It is only in Me my child, that mankind will find peace."

Has the Blessed Virgin Mary ever warned of chastisements?

In 1917, during World War I, the Blessed Virgin Mary appeared from heaven to three young children in Fatima, Portugal. She prophesied destruction as a divine judgment and punishment for sins. She said, *"War is a punishment for sins."*

She told them that if people did not change and pray, a war worse than World War I would come. She said, *"The war is going to end (World War I); but if people do not cease offending God, a worse one will break out during the pontificate of Pius XI (World War II). When you see a night illumined by an unknown light, know that this is the great sign given to you by God that He is about to punish the world for its crimes by means of war, famine and persecutions of the Church and of the Holy Father."* These prophecies were fulfilled. She also warned that if her messages were not obeyed, "nations will be annihilated."

On October 13, 1973, at Akita, Japan, Our Lady said, *"If men do not repent and better themselves, the Father will inflict a terrible punishment on all humanity. It will be a punishment greater than the deluge, such as one will never have seen before. Fire will fall from the sky and will wipe out a great part of humanity, the good as well as the bad, sparing neither priests nor faithful. The survivors will find themselves so desolate that they will envy the dead. The only arms which will remain for you will be the Rosary and the Sign left by my Son. Each day recite the prayers of the Rosary. With the Rosary, pray for the Pope, the Bishops and the priests."*

Are the apparitions of the Blessed Virgin Mary at Fatima and Akita approved by the Church?

Yes. The apparitions of the Blessed Virgin Mary at Fatima and Akita were approved by the local Bishops as supernatural events worthy of human belief. Bishop Ito of Akita declared that the apparitions there were authentic, with the approval of Cardinal Joseph Ratzinger, President Prefect of the Congregation for the Doctrine of the Faith.

Are Our Lady's warnings at Fatima and Akita the same?

Bishop Ito affirmed that the warnings of Fatima and Akita are essentially the same. He noted the following similarities:

At Fatima, Our Lady prophesied that God "is going to punish the world for its crimes." At Akita, she prophesied, "The Father will inflict a terrible punishment on all humanity."

At Fatima, Our Lady prophesied that "various nations will be annihilated." At Akita, she prophesied, "Fire will fall from the sky and will wipe out a great part of humanity."

Are Our Lady's remedies at Fatima and Akita and Jesus King's remedies the same?

At Fatima, Our Lady said, *"Say the Rosary every day."* At Akita, she said, *"Each day recite the prayers of the Rosary."*

At Fatima, Our Lady said, *"Pray a great deal and make sacrifices for sinners."* At Akita, she said, *"Pray in reparation for the sins of men."*

Jesus King said the same, *"You MUST pray and offer sacrifices! A most fearful punishment is close at hand."*

Is there any warning in the Bible, like the Akita Warning of destruction by fire?

Yes. St. Peter wrote that the godless "deliberately ignore the fact that the heavens existed of old and earth was formed out of water and through water by the Word of God, and that it was through these same factors that the world of those days was destroyed by the floodwaters. It is the same Word which is reserving the present heavens and earth for fire, keeping them until the Day of Judgment and of the destruction of sinners." (2 Peter 3:5-7).

Part Three
Protection from Chastisements

Can chastisements be averted or mitigated?

Yes. If people respond to the warning, chastisements can be averted (turned away or avoided) or mitigated (lessened in severity). For example, the prophet Jonah warned Nineveh (ancient Iraq) that it would be destroyed in forty days. But the people repented, prayed and fasted and the chastisement was averted. (See Jonah 3).

What can we do to mitigate chastisements?

"My daughter, My little one, I offer again to straying mankind, a treasure with which they may again turn aside My Just Judgment. It is My Devotion of 'Jesus King of All Nations.' I tell you most solemnly, little one, that one of the fruits of this Devotion will be the buying of more time from My Mercy in order that souls may be converted before it is too late." (*The Journal of the Devotion* 304).

To mitigate (lessen) chastisements and to help us save souls, Jesus asked us to pray His Novena Prayer and made us a promise. He asked us to pray, *"Forgive us, O Sovereign King, our sins against you. Jesus, you are a King of Mercy. We have deserved your Just Judgment. Have mercy on us, Lord, and forgive us. We trust in your Great Mercy! O most awe-inspiring King, we bow before you and pray; May your Reign, your Kingdom, be recognized on earth!"* (*The Journal of the Devotion* 29). He promised us, **"Each time you say these prayers, I will mitigate the severity of the chastisements upon your country."** (*The Journal of the Devotion* 41).

Why have Jesus and Mary warned us now?

Jesus and Mary have warned us NOW so that chastisements can be mitigated and we can make reparative prayers and sacrifices, especially the Novena in Honor of Jesus as True King, in order to save souls.

If God does not spare sinners from chastisements, does He rescue the devout?

In His will, God can rescue the devout from chastisements. St. Peter writes, "For if God did not spare the angels when they sinned, but condemned them to the chains of Tartarus and handed them over to be kept for judgment; and if He did not spare the ancient world, even though He preserved Noah, a herald or righteousness, together with seven others, when He brought a flood upon the godless world; and if He condemned the cities of Sodom and Gomorrah to destruction, reducing them to ashes, making them an example for the godless people of what is coming; and if He rescued Lot, a righteous man oppressed by the licentious conduct of unprincipled people . . . then the Lord knows how to rescue the devout from trial and to keep the unrighteous under punishment for the day of judgment...." (2 Peter 2:4-9).

Has any scientist agreed that prayer can protect us from disasters?

Dr. Neil Frank, the former head of the National Hurricane Center, said, "I accept that a storm can be stopped [through prayer]. I've known people who had incidences where you can say, yeah, this is very strange, where the weather changed just in time." Dr. Frank directed the center in Miami until 1987 and now ranks as one of the nation's leading television meteorologists.

How did Jesus King say that the chastisement of His urgent Warning could be averted?

Like Nineveh, prayer and sacrifices can avert this chastisement. That's how Jesus King said that the chastisement of His recent urgent Warning could be averted. However, He added an important element – through His Mother's mediation. Jesus said, *"Pray, pray, pray! Prayer offered to Me through My Holy Mother. Only she can avert the chastisement that now swiftly approaches. You MUST pray and offer sacrifices."*

What did Jesus King mean by prayers and sacrifices?

Jesus King did not say what He meant by prayers and sacrifice. However, He gave us the Church, His Kingdom on earth, to teach us. The Church teaches that the greatest prayer is the Mass. It also teaches the prayers of the Rosary and adoration of the Blessed Sacrament. It would seem that these prayers would be the most pleasing to Jesus especially since Pope John Paul II declared 2003 as the Year of the Rosary.

St. Michael told Jesus' secretary, *"The Most High has appointed me a particular guardian of the Most Blessed Sacrament. Let souls turn to me for renewed devotion to Our Lord in this Blessed Sacrament! He must be properly adored, loved, thanked, praised and worshipped in this the most glorious sacrament. Let souls call upon me whenever sacrileges and abominations are being committed against the Most High God in the sac-*

rament of His love." (*The Journal of the Devotion*, Nos. 84-85). So, let us turn through St. Michael and Our Lady, in answer to Jesus' plea to "pray, pray, pray!" – in front of the Blessed Sacrament.

The year 2004 is the Year of the Eucharist proclaimed by Pope John Paul II. So let's get ourselves in front of the Blessed Sacrament and let us adore, love, thank, praise and worship Jesus King of All Nations in reparation for the sacrilegious communions received by pro-abortion Catholic politicians and other pro-abortion and pro-contraception Catholics and let us also ask Him to avert the coming chastisement through His Mother's mediation.

The Church asks us to pray, fast and give alms. The Church asks us to voluntarily fast from meat on Fridays. However, we can do better than that. We can fast on bread and water, as the state of our health may allow, and fast from enjoyments such as television, computer time, excessive work and play and make acts of mercy for others and give alms to the poor.

As Pope John Paul II said, "Jesus Himself has shown us by His own example that prayer and fasting are the first and most effective weapons against the forces of evil." (Pope John Paul II, Encyclical Letter, *The Gospel of Life,* 100). So let us pray and fast to avert the threatened chastisement.

Why should the Rosary be revived now?

In his Apostolic Letter, *On the Most Holy Rosary*, Pope John Paul II said, "A number of historical circumstances make a revival of the Rosary quite timely. First of all, *the need to implore from God the gift of peace.* At the start of a millennium which began with the terrifying attacks of September 11, 2001, a millennium which witnesses every day in numerous parts of the world fresh scenes of bloodshed and violence, to rediscover the Rosary means to immerse oneself in contemplation of the mystery of Christ who "is our peace," since He made "the two of us one, and broke down the dividing wall of hostility." (Ephesians 2:14).

What are the Rosary's Luminous Mysteries?

Pope John Paul II added the Luminous Mysteries (Mysteries of Light) so that we can meditate on Jesus' public ministry. He said, "In proposing to the Christian community five significant moments 'the luminous mysteries' during this phase of Christ's life, I think that the following can be fittingly singled out: (1) His Baptism in the Jordan, (2) His self-manifestation at the wedding of Cana, (3) His proclamation of the Kingdom of God, with His call to conversion, (4) His Transfiguration, and finally, (5) His institution of the Eucharist, as the sacramental expression of the Paschal Mystery."

The Holy Father entrusted to the power of the Rosary the cause of peace in the world and the cause of the family. He said, "Confidently take up the Rosary once again. . . . **May this appeal of mine not go unheard!**" (Pope John Paul II, *On the Most Holy Rosary).*

How did Pope John Paul II close the Year of the Rosary?

He prayed the Rosary on the Feast of the Rosary in the Year of the Rosary at the Shrine of the Rosary in Pompeii, Italy. Each one of the five mysteries was dedicated to the peace of a continent. Representatives of Europe, Asia, Africa, the Americas and Oceania went to the platform to light a candle before the image of Our Lady of the Rosary.

The Holy Father said, "We have meditated on the mysteries of light, as though wishing to project the light of Christ on the conflicts, tensions and dramas of the five continents."

Did Pompeii suffer from a chastisement?

The Shrine of the Virgin of the Rosary in Pompeii was built next to the famous ancient Roman city buried by a volcano. Pompeii was destroyed in 79 A.D. when nearby Mount Vesuvius erupted and covered the city in volcanic ash and debris. Many believe that this was a divine chastisement for the sins of ancient pagan Pompeii and the Pope hinted at this in his talk.

The Holy Father said, "Today's visit is, in a certain sense, the crowning of the Year of the Rosary. . . . This prayer, simple but profound, touches the heart of the Christian faith and is extremely relevant, given the challenges of the third millennium and the urgent commitment to the new evangelization.

"In Pompeii," he continued, "this relevance is highlighted in a particular way in the context of the ancient Roman city, buried under the ashes of Vesuvius in A.D. 79. **These ruins speak. They pose the decisive question on the destiny of man.** They are testimony of a great culture of which they reveal, along with luminous answers, disturbing questions. The Marian city is born at the heart of these questions, presenting the risen Christ as the answer, as the Gospel that saves."

We all should heed the Holy Father's appeal to "confidently take up the Rosary once again" in order to mitigate chastisements.

What promise did Jesus King give us to protect us from chastisements?

Jesus King said, *"I promise to offer the grace of protection in times of harm and danger. This will especially be true of danger coming from natural disasters."*

23

What special prayer did Jesus King give us to protect us from chastisements?

The Novena Prayer in Honor of Jesus King of All Nations that is contained in the Appendix. He told us to pray to Him "in the great expectation of receiving from you O Divine King, mercy, peace, justice and all good things." He asked us to pray to Him to "protect our families and the land of our birth, guard us Most Faithful One, protect us from our enemies and from your just judgment." He promised us, *"Each time you say these Novena prayers, I will mitigate the severity of the chastisements upon your country."*

How can prayers and sacrifices bring strength and peace?

Our Lady requested prayers and sacrifices for conversions and peace at Fatima, Portugal in 1917. She said, "Will you offer yourselves to God, and bear all the sufferings He sends you in atonement for all the sins that offend Him and for the conversion of sinners? The grace of God will be with you and will strengthen you. Say the Rosary every day to bring peace to the world."

Who alone can save us from Jesus' urgent Warning of chastisement?

Jesus said, *"Only [my Mother] can avert the chastisement that now swiftly approaches."*

Our Lady of Akita, Japan, told Sister Agnes in 1973, *"I alone am able still to save you from the calamities that approach. Those who place their confidence in me will be saved."*

Does the Blessed Virgin Mary intercede for us in heaven?

Yes. In her motherly love Mary intercedes with Jesus to care for us on earth. The Church teaches that, "Taken up to heaven she did not lay aside this saving office but by her manifold intercession continues to bring us the gifts of eternal salvation. By her maternal charity, she cares for the brethren of her Son, who still journey on earth surrounded by dangers and difficulties, until they are led into their blessed home." (Vatican Council II, *Dogmatic Constitution of the Church* 61-62). That is why we pray through her mediation.

What did Jesus King mean by offering prayer "through My Holy Mother?"

Mediation means to "go between" two parties. Jesus asks that we use His Mother as a "go between" Him and us. The sole mediator between God and humanity is Jesus who gave Himself as a ransom for all. (See 1 Timothy 2:5-6). A mediator is a friendly third party who interposes between parties who are not united. Jesus is our mediator with God because He shared our human nature so that we could share His divine nature through the graces merited by His passion and death.

However, the Blessed Virgin Mary is also a subordinate mediator between Jesus and us through her intercession and the dispensation of the graces merited by Him. She mediates all graces to us form God and she also mediates to God from us all of our prayers, sacrifices and good works. That is why she is called the Mediatrix of All Graces and that is why Jesus King asked us to pray "through My Holy Mother."

What does the title, "Mary Mediatrix of All Graces" mean?

The title, "Mary Mediatrix of All Graces" means that Mary is the channel of graces from the Father to us merited by her Son. Grace is the very life of God, which is communicated to us from the Father. It is simply the will of Almighty God to exercise the power of Christ's mediation by the application of His merited graces to us through the mediation of His Mother.

Pope John Paul II said, "Mary places herself between her Son and mankind in the reality of their wants, needs and suffering. She puts herself 'in the middle,' that is to say she acts as a mediatrix, not as an outsider, but in her position as Mother. She knows that as such she can point out to her Son the needs of mankind, and in fact, she 'has the right' to do so." (Pope John Paul II, Encyclical Letter, *Mother of the Redeemer*.).

What did Jesus King say about Mary as the Mediatrix of All Grace?

Jesus asks those who embrace His devotion as King of All Nations to consecrate themselves to His Mother under her title as "Mary, Mediatrix of All Grace." His servant recorded Jesus' words.

"My beloved little daughter, your Lord and God comes to you to give you a message of great importance. I desire that the souls who embrace My devotion to 'Jesus King of All Nations,' make a special consecration to My Most Holy Mother under her title of 'Mary Mediatrix of All Grace,' which it has pleased Me in My Great Love for her to give her. People MUST acknowledge her indispensable role as the Mediatrix, the Channel,

of all of My Graces to mankind. Only when this dogma is officially pro-claimed by My Church will I truly establish My Reign on earth."

By this consecration we ask Mary to receive us and to present us and our every need to the Most Holy Trinity! That having been made pure and holy in His Sight through her hands, they may return to us, through her, as graces and blessing. This Consecration is contained in the Appendix.

Part Four
Warnings and Chastisements for America

What was Jesus' warning to Jerusalem?

Jesus warned Jerusalem of its destruction, but the people did not listen and Jerusalem was annihilated. Jesus prophesied that not a stone upon a stone would be left in Jerusalem because they did not recognize the path to peace. (See Luke 19:41-44). This prophecy was literally fulfilled in the year 70 A.D. by the Roman General Titus who destroyed the city. This warning is similar to the urgent warning of Jesus King of All Nations of the destruction of cities.

What is the chastisement of Jesus' urgent Warning of August 25, 2004?

Jesus King of All Nations said, *"A most fearful punishment is close at hand .Cities will be simultaneously affected. Great destruction, great loss of life. Great sorrow and pain. Smoke and fire. Wailing and lamentation."*

What were Pope John Paul II's warnings to America?

In 1976, the Holy Father (as Cardinal Wojtyla) while in the United States warned us, "We are now standing in the face of the greatest historical confrontation humanity has gone through. I do not think that wide circles of the American society, or wide circles of the Christian community, realize this fully. We are now facing the FINAL CONFRONTATION between the Church and the anti-Church, of the Gospel versus the anti-Gospel."

In 1979, the Holy Father stood in front of the United States Supreme Court justices who had "legalized" abortion and said, "When the sacredness of life before birth is attacked, we will STAND UP and proclaim that no one ever has the authority to destroy unborn life."

In 1987, the Holy Father issued another warning to America when he left Detroit. "This is the dignity of America, the reason she exists, THE CONDITION FOR HER SURVIVAL – yes, the ultimate test of her greatness: to respect every human person, especially the weakest and most defenseless ones, those as yet unborn."

In 1993 at World Youth Day in Denver, the Holy Father once again warned America. He said, "If you want equal justice for all, lasting justice and peace, America: Defend life. America needs much prayer . . . lest it lose its soul. Do not be afraid to go out on the streets and into public places, like the first apostles. This is no time to be ashamed of the Gospel.

It is the time to preach it from the rooftops. Do not be afraid to break out of comfortable and routine modes of living, in order to take up the challenge of making Christ known in the modern metropolis. . . . America, defend life so that you may live in peace and harmony. **Woe to you if you do not succeed in defending life**."

These are the most severe prophetic warnings that America has ever received. The Holy Father tells us that the very condition for our nation's survival is to end abortion. He uses the warning words of the prophets, "Woe to you . . . ."

What analogy did Pope John II make between slavery and abortion in America?

In 1855, President Lincoln said, "Can we, as a nation, continue together permanently – forever half slave and half free? The problem is too mighty for me. May God, in His mercy, superintend the solution."

One hundred and forty years later, Pope John Paul II said, "President Lincoln's question is no less a question for the present generation of Americans. Democracy cannot be sustained without a shared commitment to certain moral truths about the human person and human community." (Pope John Paul II, Address, October 1995). Can we continue together as a nation permanently – forever half pro-abortion and half pro-life?

What did Pope John Paul II say is America's role in the Third Millennium?

As the prophets of old, Pope John Paul II called the Church in America to conversion by "a profound interior renewal through a revitalization of missionary zeal."

The Holy Father stressed "the importance of the evangelization of culture" especially "the new global culture which is rapidly taking shape as a result of unprecedented growth in communications and the expansion of a world economy. I am convinced," he said, " that the Church in the United States can play a critical role in meeting this challenge. . . ."

He said,

> For the Church in America, the evangelization of culture can thus offer a unique contribution to the Church's mission *ad gentes* (to the nations) in our day. . . . Catholics of all ages must be helped to appreciate more fully the distinctiveness of the Christian message, its capacity to satisfy the deepest yearnings of the human heart in every

age, and the beauty of its summons to a life completely centered on faith in the Triune God, obedience to His revealed word and loving configuration to Christ's paschal mystery, in which we see disclosed the full measure of our humanity and our supernatural call to fulfillment in love. (See, Documents of Vatican Council II, *Gaudium et Spes*, 22).

. . . . As the tragic events of 11 September 2001 have made clear, the building of a global culture of solidarity and respect for human dignity is one of the great moral tasks confronting humanity today. In the end, it is in the conversion of hearts and the spiritual renewal of humanity that the hope of a better tomorrow lies, and here the witness, example and cooperation of religious believers have a unique role to play. . . .

May the Church in your country discover the sources for a profound interior renewal through a revitalization of missionary zeal, above all by promoting vocations to missionary Institutes and proposing, especially to young people, the lofty ideal of a life completely devoted to the Gospel. . . . (Pope John Paul II, Address to U.S. Bishops of Boston and Hartford, September 2, 2004).

Was America saved from the chastisement of nuclear war?

Yes. Sister Lucia, the last surviving visionary of Our Lady of Fatima, revealed that the world was saved from nuclear war "that would have occurred in 1985" if Pope John Paul II had not made the collegial consecration of the world in 1984 to the Immaculate Heart of Mary, as she requested at Fatima, Portugal.

Did Jesus King avert a threatened chastisement to America?

Yes. In answer to the prayers of the Devotion, Jesus averted a chastisement that He had prophesied. Jesus had prophesied a seaquake for Puerto Rico as a punishment for its sins. A seaquake is an earthquake below sea level that can cause devastating tidal waves and destruction. In response to the prophecy, high officials of the Church and the government of Puerto Rico turned to Jesus and personally prayed the devotional prayers for mercy and to avert the threatened chastisement.

Jesus heard their prayers and averted the chastisement. He said, *"Some have received me as their Lord and King in the Devotion that I have given you to give to the world, that of 'Jesus, King of All Nations.' My message was received with an open heart and with an open soul and they did not receive you with scorn or indifference or mock the messages that I have sent, or refuse to listen! I have shown them that if they turn to me, their Merciful King who desires to reign in their hearts, that I am a King of Mercy, a Father of Mercy, a Lord of Love who does not want their unnecessary deaths and condemnation of their souls because of their sins and stubbornness in pride."*

Did Jesus King warn America to wake us up?

Yes. After He averted the Puerto Rican chastisement, Jesus said that if we don't wake up and see the lightning of His mercy, we will experience the thunder of His justice (chastisement).

He said, *"Have No Doubt – The Thunder Of My Justice Was Going TO Be Heard!!! As thunder comes before the rain, so the thunder of my just judgment upon them was going to be heard first! Will my children WAKE UP and see the lightning first? The lightning of merciful rays of my Mercy that I wish to strike their hearts with!"*

"Will they notice me who Am? Will my people finally see with the light of my grace so that I can reign in their hearts?! Yes, I wish to be the Light that comes before the reign! The reign of my Merciful Kingship! Choose my people; choose how you wish to serve me!"

"It is you my special little ones who have found the fulfillment of my promises not only for yourselves, but for your whole nation! Remember what I have done for you my people, of how I have spared you this time!"

Was Hurricane Charley averted in any way?

Yes. It was 3:30 p.m. on Friday, August 14, 2004 during the hour of Mercy. I gathered with my staff in our chapel in our Vermont apostolate center. We turned to St Michael and prayed, "St. Michael, Great Prince and Guardian of your people, come with the holy angels and saints and protect us!" We also prayed the Chaplet of Unity for protection and the Chaplet of Mercy for the victims. Hurricane Charley was approaching directly upon our small branch office in a mobile home park in Nokomis, on the west coast of Florida.

Jesus King of All Nations promised for those who practice His Devotion "protection in times of harm and danger. This will especially be true of danger coming from natural disasters."

This was certainly a danger from a natural disaster and we prayed in earnest for protection of our office. As we prayed, the hurricane inexplicably took a right turn, and at 3:45 p.m. it hit land with a ferocious force just 25 miles south of our office. The hurricane totally wiped out many mobile home parks but left ours with just a little wind and rain. Not even a branch fell!

I attribute this protection to Jesus King of All Nations and to St. Michael. I encourage you to buy *The Journal* and read all of Jesus' promises for protection. Many more natural disasters will be coming as God continues to warn humanity of its errant ways and speaks to us loudly through the voice of nature.

Why do militant Muslim terrorists hate Americans?

Osama Bin Laden himself tells us the reasons in his 1996 "Declaration of War Against the Americans Occupying the Land of the Two Holy Places."

He and his followers are at war to kill all the "infidels" (Americans) and their allies. He especially hates the Jews of Israel who he thinks "stole" Arab land.

He wants to restore Islam to the power it had during the Middle Ages.

He wants the United States and all "infidels" to be excluded from the Muslim holy lands of Saudi Arabia and Iraq because they desecrate the land.

He wants to end the effects upon Muslims of America's materialism and moral depravity. Islam teaches modesty, sexual purity for both women and men and respect for life. Western culture's moral depravity comes to Muslims through the media of movies, music and the Internet.

What should our individual attitude be toward terrorists?

We should not harbor personal thoughts of retaliation and revenge but remember the words of Jesus who said to his disciples, "Love your enemies, do good to those who hate you, bless those who curse you, pray for those who mistreat you." (Luke 6-27-28).

Was 9/11 prophesied?

Exactly two years before The Attack on America, on September 11, 1999, I stood with Irish mystic Christina Gallagher in Battery Park, New York City at the tip of Manhattan Island in the shadows of the World Trade Center. I remarked on the enormity of the twin World Trade Towers as a symbol of America's economic might and our reliance on the priority of power over prayer. As I said this, Christina waved her arm towards the Twin Towers and prophesied, "Dan, all of this will be destroyed!"

On September 12th, 2001 Christina personally confirmed to me that on September 11, 1999, <u>she prophesied the disastrous destruction of the Twin Towers.</u>

Was the prophecy fulfilled?

Christina told me "*all* of this will be destroyed" as she waved her arm towards the Twin Towers. In fact not just the Twin Towers, but *all* 14 buildings as high as 44 stories over 4 square city blocks were destroyed.

Was the 9/11 prophecy a message from God?

On September 12, 2002, Christina Gallagher announced in a newspaper interview, "I responded to a remark that (Judge Dan Lynch) made. I knew nothing about the Twin Towers except what God gave me. It was a divine message."

Was 9/11 a chastisement?

We should acknowledge that God's justice, through the hands of malevolent terrorists, was brought to us because of our legalized abortions, embryonic experimentation and homosexual unions. God has allowed this chastisement because of our failure to trust in Him and His ways. It was an emergency wake-up call for America. September 11 (9/11) is symbolic of the 911 emergency phone number for America! We must listen to the call of the modern day prophets to repent, convert, pray, fast and receive the sacraments of Confession and the Eucharist! Then we will be reconciled with God – the God who loves us and doesn't want our condemnation but our salvation. (See John 3:17).

Our trust and security is not in our economic might (symbolized by the destroyed Twin Towers) or our military might (symbolized by the damaged Pentagon). As our national motto says, "In God we trust." We must trust God to bring goodness out of this great evil.

Does God chastise nations?

Abraham Lincoln recognized that God's justice is brought upon nations as well as individuals. In the middle of the Civil War, on March 30, 1863, he said, "We know that by His divine law nations, like individuals, are subjected to punishments and chastisements in this world."

God is merciful but He is also just. His justice can be brought to nations through wars and natural disasters resulting in suffering of the guilty as well as the innocent. This suffering is mysteriously meritorious to those who accept it, abandon themselves and offer it to God. Suffering also brings us to repentance that brings God's merciful forgiveness, healing and union with Him.

The purpose of God's justice is not to condemn us but to redeem us. He tries every means to win the love of sinners who initially reject Him. In our Lord Jesus, the most innocent, we see how far He goes. "For God so loved the world that He gave His only Son." (John 3:16).

Did God say that He would heal us from chastisements?

Yes. God said, "When I shut up the heavens so that there is no rain, or command the locust to devour the land, or send pestilence among my people, if my people who are called by my name humble themselves, and pray and seek my face, and turn from their wicked ways, then I will hear from heaven, and will forgive their sin and heal their land." (2 Chronicles 7:13-14).

Did any American President recognize that we must humble ourselves and pray?

Abraham Lincoln recognized that our country had to humble itself and pray. On March 30, 1863, in the middle of the Civil War, he proclaimed a National Day of Prayer and Fasting. He said, "It is the duty of nations, as well as of men to own their dependence on the overruling power of God; to confess their sins and transgressions in humble sorrow, yet with assured hope that genuine repentance will lead to mercy and pardon. . . . And insomuch as we know that by His divine law nations, like individuals, are subjected to punishments and chastisements in this world, may we not justly fear that the awful calamity of civil war which now desolates the land may be but a punishment inflicted upon us for our presumptuous sins, to the needful end of our national reformation as a whole people? . . . Intoxicated with unbroken success, we have become too self-sufficient to feel the necessity of redeeming and preserving grace, too proud to pray to the God that made us. . . . It behooves us, then, to humble ourselves before the offended Power, to confess our national sins, and to pray for clemency and forgiveness."

These words apply to us even more forcefully today as we remain at war in Iraq and with militant Muslim terrorists.

Why are there so many American disasters?

Many people today wonder about so many disasters just as did the prophet Jeremiah. He said, "Why is all this happening to me? It is because of the grossness of your sins . . . ." (Jeremiah 13:22).

Why is all this happening to us? The ten worst disasters in the history of the United States all occurred in the last ten years of the 20th century. Why so many disasters? For the same reason, the grossness of our sins – the grossness of abortion, embryonic experimentation and homosexual unions.

The disasters are listed as follows by year with their losses in billions of 2002 dollars:

1. 2001 World Trade Center, Pentagon attacks	$40.63
2. 1992 Hurricane Andrew	$19.87
3. 1994 Northridge California Earthquake	$15.17
4. 1989 Hurricane Hugo	$ 6.08
5. 1998 Hurricane Georges	$ 3.20
6. 2001 Tropical Storm Allison	$ 2.54
7. 1995 Hurricane Opal	$ 2.48
8. 1999 Hurricane Floyd	$ 2.12
9. 1993 20-state winter storm	$ 2.21
10. 1991 Oakland California wildfire	$ 2.24

What is the Remedy?

Jesus King said, *"I have come to entrust to you a message of great importance for the world. I tell you . . . the days are coming when Mankind will cry out to Me for mercy. I tell you, My child, only one thing will be given as a remedy. I Myself AM that remedy! Let souls give devotion to Me through My Most Holy Mother, who mediates to Me on their behalf, as 'Jesus King of All Nations.' "*

Does the liturgy offer any prayers to avert natural disasters?

Yes. The altar missal includes a "Procession for Averting Tempest." It begins with church bells, a litany of the saints and the following:
"Almighty and ever living God, spare us in our anxiety and take pity on us in our abasement, so that after the lightning in the skies and the force of the storm have calmed, even the very threat of tempest may be an occasion for us to offer You praise. Lord Jesus, Who uttered a word of command to the raging tempest of wind and sea and there came a great calm: hear the prayers of Your family."

Were the victims of the 9/11 Twin Towers disaster guilty?

Not necessarily. It's like Jesus said about the victims of the destruction of the Tower of Siloam. He was asked if they were guilty. He replied, "Certainly not! But I tell you, unless you repent, you will all perish as they did." (Luke 13:5). We too must repent to avoid the same end.

The greatest act of God's justice was upon Jesus Himself, the God-Man who was a totally innocent victim. He took upon Himself the punishment for all of our sins in order to save us and grant us the gift of eternal life through the forgiveness of our sins.

Where was God at Ground Zero?

Many people ask, "Where was God at Ground Zero?" God's protection was lessened on 9/11 because of America's institutionalized evils of legally protected abortion and homosexual unions. However, the chastisement was also lessened. It could have been much worse. Approximately ½ of the workers in the Twin Towers were absent and of those present 25,000 safely left the buildings.

God mercifully allowed many people enough time to prepare for death. One woman called her mother and said, "Mom, I'm about to die, what do I do?" Over the phone, her mother calmly led her in the Act of Contrition.

In fact, God was at Ground Zero. He was there in the presence of all the rescuers and helpers who practiced the works of mercy – feeding the hungry, giving drink to the thirsty, burying the dead and comforting the sorrowful. Jesus said, "Whatsoever you do the to the least of my children, you do to me."

The workers of mercy said that there was such a feeling of peace and unity that it could only be ascribed to the presence of the Holy Sprit who brings such gifts. Only the Holy Sprit can bring such good out of such tremendous evil amidst such great human suffering. We are all called to "depart from evil, and do good; seek peace and pursue it." (Psalm 34:14).

The rescuers were loving, patient and kind which are gifts of the Holy Sprit. Brother firefighters and police were there along with volunteers who drove hundreds of miles to help. Police officers greeted visitors at Ground Zero with smiles, volunteers cheerfully offered water and snacks. All worked for the common good of all as guided by the Sprit of love.

Part Five
Hope for the Future

Are there any hopeful signs?

Mary is the Mother of Hope. She is the Mother of Jesus Christ who is our hope as the conqueror of sin and death. As a people of hope, we are not afraid but look forward to the victory of good over evil; peace over war; truth over lies; love over hate and life over death. We look forward to eternal salvation and an existence full of happiness in God.

Hope is the confident expectation of divine blessing. (*Catechism of the Catholic Church* 1818). Our Lady of Guadalupe said that she is the Mother "of all those who have confidence in me." Through her, we should have confidence in divine blessings. That is hope.

Has Pope John Paul II recognized any signs of hope in the world?

Pope John Paul II said, "With full confidence let us place under the vigilant intercession of Holy Mary . . . . the prospect of the Third Millennium. The Third Millennium remains for us a horizon of very stimulating reflections, because it makes us look forward in hope. The Blessed Mary is the guide in the new exodus towards the future."

Hope in the abstract is realized by signs in today's world recognized by Pope John Paul II in his Apostolic Letter, *On the Coming of the Third Millennium*. He said, "In civil society, such signs are the progress that has been made by science, technology, and especially medicine in serving human life; the keener sense of responsibility toward the environment; the efforts to reestablish peace and justice wherever they have been violated; the resolute desire for reconciliation and solidarity among peoples, especially in the complex relations between the North and South of the world. . . .In the Church, such signs are more attentive listening to the voice of the Spirit through the acceptance of charisms and the promotion of the laity; intense devotion to the cause of unity on the part of individual Christians; the space given to dialogue with the religions and with contemporary culture."

Only God knows what the future holds. But we are certain that He is the Lord of history and directs it to His own end with our cooperation in hope. It will be the fulfillment of a divine plan of love for all humanity and for each one of us. "That is why," the Holy Father said, "as we look into the future, we are full of hope and are not overcome with fear. The journey . . . is a great journey of hope."

The Pope also said, "As the third millennium of the redemption draws near, God is preparing a great springtime for Christianity, and we can already see its first signs. . . . Christian hope sustains us in committing ourselves fully to the New Evangelization and to the worldwide mission, and leads us to pray as Jesus taught us: "Thy will be done, on earth as it is in heaven." (Matthew 6:10). (Pope John Paul II, Encyclical Letter, *Mission of the Redeemer* 86).

This hope reminds us of Our Lady of Guadalupe's assurance to Saint Juan Diego, "Do not fear any illness or vexation, anxiety or pain. Am I not here who am your Mother? Am I not your hope?" Our Lady of Guadalupe is the Star of the New Evangelization and, as our Mother of Hope, she leads us in hope as we entrust ourselves with all of our hearts to God's great and generous promises of eternal life and happiness with Him.

In his Apostolic Letter, *On the Coming of the Third Millennium,* the Holy Father closed his remarks and said, "Christians are called to prepare . . . . by renewing their hope in the definitive coming of the kingdom of God, preparing for it daily in their hearts in the Christian community to which they belong, in their particular social context, and in the world history itself."

Let us pray and act for the fulfillment of the Holy Father's prophecy, "Through Our Lady of Guadalupe's powerful intercession, the Gospel will penetrate the hearts of the men and women of America and permeate their cultures, transforming them from within."

What is the mission and power of the Blessed Virgin Mary?

Our Lady's mission and power from the beginning as granted by God has been to crush the head of Satan. (See Genesis 3:15). She told Father Gobbi, *"I am the victorious Woman. In the end, the power of Satan will be destroyed, and I myself will bind him with my chain and I will shut him up within his kingdom of death and of eternal torment, from which he will not be able to get out. In the world, there will reign the one and only conqueror of sin and of death, the king of the entire created universe, Jesus Christ."*

Jesus has empowered us to help Our Lady to bring the victory and the triumph of her Immaculate Heart in the world today that will usher in His reign as Jesus King of All Nations. He said, "I have observed Satan fall like lightning from the sky. Behold, I have given you power to tread upon serpents and scorpions and upon the full force of the enemy and nothing will harm you." (Luke 10:18-19).

What is the Triumph of the Immaculate Heart of Mary?

The Triumph of the Immaculate Heart of Mary was first prophesied by Our Lady of Fatima on July 13, 1917 when she told the three children, "In the end my Immaculate Heart will triumph. The Holy Father will consecrate Russia to me and she will be converted, and an era of peace will be granted to the world."

The Triumph of the Immaculate Heart of Mary began with Pope John Paul II's collegial consecration of the World to her Immaculate Heart on March 25, 1984. This Triumph is an ongoing process.

What did Jesus King say about the Triumph of the Immaculate Heart of Mary?

Jesus King said, *"My Most Holy Mother is preparing the great triumph. The Triumph of her Immaculate Heart ushers in the Reign of My Love and Mercy."* (*The Journal of the Devotion* 14).

This is the Reign of the Kingdom of God. In the Holy Father's Apostolic Letter, *On the Coming of the Third Millennium*, he said that **the virtue of hope is aimed at "the definitive coming of the Kingdom of God."**

The reign of this Kingdom is a new mystery of the Luminous Mysteries of the Rosary. The Holy Father announced these new mysteries to give us a weapon to usher in the reign of Christ's Kingdom at a time when Satan seems to reign through chastisements of terrorism, war, serial murders, famine, natural disasters and the moral breakdown of families and society in a Culture of Death that legalizes pornography, abortion and homosexual unions but makes the presence of Christ the King illegal in our public institutions.

What is the New Era of Peace?

On July 13, 1917, Our Lady of Fatima told the three children, *"An era of peace will be granted to the world."* Sister Lucia, one of the children, later said, "The period of peace does not refer to civil peace." This peace is not merely the absence of external conflict. It is a positive interior quality, which is a gift from Jesus (see John 14:27) beginning in our hearts and flowing out to others. It is God's own peace, which is beyond all understanding. (See Philippians 4:7). This peace will be a gift from God and not earned by human effort, imposed by political effort or gained by any human means whatsoever. This peace is not obtainable without responding to Jesus' plea for conversion, prayer and sacrifice. It is the peace that Pope John Paul II prayed for at the Basilica of Our Lady of Guadalupe, "with the peace of God in our conscience, with our hearts free from evil and hatred we will be able to bring to all true joy and true peace, which comes to us from your Son, our Lord Jesus Christ, who with God the Father and the Holy Spirit lives and reigns for ever and ever. Amen."

How has Pope John Paul II described the New Era?

Pope John Paul II said, "I once more express my conviction, born of faith, that God is even now preparing a great springtime for the Gospel (see *Redemptoris Missio*, 86) . . . ." (Pope John Paul II, Address to U.S. Bishops of Boston and Hartford, September 2. 2004).

He said that in the New Era brought by Christ, "God and man, man and woman, humanity and nature are in harmony, in dialogue, in communion."

The authentic New Era is nothing other than the re-establishment of the lost relation between God and man. The Holy Father said, "Christ must cancel the work of devastation, the horrible idolatry, violence and every sin that the rebellious Adam has spread in the secular affairs of humanity and on the horizon of creation.

"He 'recapitulates' Adam in himself, in whom the whole of humanity recognizes itself; he transfigures him into Son of God, he brings him to full communion with the Father," the Pope explained.

Christ's New Era also embraces "nature itself . . . subjected as it is to lack of meaning, degradation and devastation caused by sin," which will thus participate "in the joy of the deliverance brought about by Christ in the Holy Spirit." (Pope John Paul II, General Audience, Feb 14, 2001). Spreading the Devotion to Jesus King of All Nations will help to bring this New Era.

How should we await this New Era?

We confidently await this New Era in hope. We recall Pope Pius XII's expression of confidence in Our Lady of Guadalupe when he said, "We are certain that as long as you are recognized as Queen and as Mother, the Americas and Mexico will be safe." We recall Our Lady of Guadalupe's promise to Juan Diego that she would show her help and protection to the people.

Will there be a worldwide Warning and Chastisement before this New Era of Peace?

Hope for the New Era of Peace cannot be realized without God's purification of the world through a worldwide Warning and Chastisement.

The many mystics in the world today tell us that chastisements will

God. These will lead up to a time of a worldwide Warning. At the same moment everywhere on the earth, God will reveal to every human being the state of his or her soul before Him. There will be a great illumination of conscience. Each person will experience the enlightenment of their souls, they will know all of their sins and they will see the state of their souls as God sees them. It will be like His judgment at the moment of death except that there will be a merciful opportunity to convert. There will be an illuminated Cross of light and many more signs to help the disbelievers believe that these signs are from God. But by this time it may be too late for many to permanently convert and they may lapse away from grace and back into sin.

Will there be a Sign before the worldwide Chastisement?

Jesus told Saint Faustina, *"Before I come as the just judge, I am coming first as the King of Mercy. Before the day of justice arrives, there will be given to people a sign in the heavens of this sort: 'All light in the heavens will be extinguished, and there will be great darkness over the whole earth. Then the sign of the Cross will be seen in the sky, and from the openings where the hands and the feet of the Savior were nailed will come forth great lights which will light up the earth for a period of time. This will take place shortly before the last day.' "* (Saint Faustina's Diary, *Divine Mercy in My Soul* 83).

Will there be a worldwide Chastisement after the Warning and the Sign?

After the Warning, a Chastisement will come which will purify the world and wipe it clean of sin.

Jesus revealed to His "Secretary," *"Now is the time of Great Mercy. Take heed and benefit from it. If you do not, a most grievous Chastisement will suddenly fall upon you."* (*The Journal of the Devotion* 23).

What is the purpose of the worldwide Chastisement?

Our Lady told Father Gobbi of the Marian Movement of Priests that the purpose of the Chastisement is the purification and renewal of the world and the salvation of souls. Jesus will live again in the hearts of humanity and through us He will act, work, love, suffer, die and rise to a new life in His Church so that He will "present to Himself a glorious Church, holy, and immaculate, without stain or wrinkle or anything of that sort." (Ephesians 5:27). Jesus will reign in a universal reign of grace, of beauty, of harmony, of communion, of sanctity, and of justice and peace, all of which will be established in the world and will shine forth resplendently in the hearts of all."

What did Jesus King say about a worldwide Chastisement?

Jesus revealed to His "Secretary," *"No, my beloved, sin and the evils committed by mankind are too great, no longer will I spare my judgment to correct the conscience of mankind as a whole, but this Devotion prayed with repentance, confidence, and love, will heal, save, and unite souls to my mercy who otherwise would be lost."* (*The Journal of the Devotion* 55).

Did Jesus King reveal a vision of the worldwide Chastisement?

The other mystic of the Devotion is known as the "Spiritual Mother," because that is her relationship to Jesus' Secretary. Once the Spiritual Mother had a vision of Jesus King of All Nations. She said, **"He let me behold a Heavenly Chastisement, which is to come. Greater than any Hiroshima could ever be.** (Hiroshima is in Japan where the first atomic bomb was dropped). It was a merciful calling from God; a Chastisement of mercy because God's people's hearts were far from Him and they no longer revered Him as God. I am speaking this because God asked me to say this to His people. **Repent! Come and be healed in the Sacrament of Confession.** Come and be healed by asking for forgiveness. Come and be healed with the Merciful Love that God offers us." (*The Journal of the Devotion* 147-148).

Were people who prayed protected from the atomic bomb?

Yes. Takashi Nagai survived the second atomic blast at Nagasaki, Japan. He was only 1000 yards from ground zero and survived, just like the priests nearby who had promoted devotion to the Rosary. Takashi's experience gives an objective reality on a *smaller* scale of Jesus' warning vision above of a *greater* chastisement, "greater than any Hiroshima could ever be."

Takashi said, "There was a flash of blinding light. A giant hand seemed to grab me and hurl me three meters. The giant invisible fist had gone berserk and was smashing everything in the office and I listened to strange noises like mountains rumbling back and forth. Then came pitch darkness. Panic gripped my heart when I heard crackling flames and sniffed acrid smoke. I was conscious of my sins and directed my whole attention to the Lord our Judge and asked His forgiveness."

How did an atomic bomb survivor characterize the innocent victims?

Survivor Takashi Nagai characterized the innocent victims as a great sacrificial offering to restore peace. Takashi gave an exhortation at an outdoor Requiem Mass for the atomic bomb victims later said by the Bishop among the rubble of his former cathedral. He said, "In order to restore peace to the world it was not sufficient to repent. We had to obtain God's pardon through the offering of a great sacrifice . . . . Only a remnant has survived. In the midst of the ruins we stand in groups of two or three looking blankly at the sky . . . . And as we walk in hunger and thirst, ridiculed, penalized, scourged, pouring with sweat and covered with blood, let us remember that Jesus Christ carried His Cross to the hill of Calvary. He will give us courage."

Let us have the courage of Takashi and pray the Novena to Christ the King to avert and mitigate chastisements.

Should we be afraid?

No. This is no time to be afraid! Jesus said, "Fear is useless, what is needed is trust." (Mark 5:36).

Saint John the Evangelist said, "We should have confidence for the day of judgment. . . ." (1 John 4:17). "There is no fear in love, but perfect love casts out fear. For fear has to do with punishment, and he who fears is not perfected in love." (1 John 4:18).

Our Lady of Akita told Sister Agnes in the 1970s, *"I alone am able still to save you from the calamities that approach. Those who place their confidence in me will be saved."*

In His urgent Warning, Jesus King of All Nations quoted scripture. "Fear not, be not troubled." (Isaiah 44:6-8).

Our Lady of Guadalupe told St. Juan Diego, *"I am your merciful mother, listen and let it penetrate your heart, do not be troubled or weighed down with grief. Do not fear any illness or vexation, anxiety or pain. Am I not here who am your Mother? Are you not under my shadow and protection?"*

How can we trust?

John Paul II offered personal counsel when facing times of difficulty – the invocation "Jesus, I trust in you." "It is a simple but profound act of trust and abandonment to the love of God," the Pope said. "It is a fundamental point of strength for every man, as it is capable of transforming life."

"In the inevitable trials and difficulties of life, in moments of joy and enthusiasm, entrusting oneself to the Lord infuses the soul with peace, induces us to recognize the primacy of the divine initiative and opens the spirit to humility and trust," he added. (John Paul II, Meeting with Students of the Major Seminary of the Rome Diocese, March 3, 2003.)

What will happen after the worldwide Chastisement?

After the Chastisement, the Immaculate Heart of Mary will Triumph and there will be an Era of Peace. This Triumph will bring the Reign of the Kingdom of God and the New Era. In the meantime, we are called to prayer, sacrifice and the sacraments to mitigate the chastisements through Our Lady's mediation.

What good is it to pray if the worldwide Chastisement is coming anyway?

Jesus said, *"Do you know, My little one, that if it were not for the love of the faithful few, My Father would have long ago destroyed the earth which is full of the guilt of sin? My Child, make known this truth to My faithful children, so that they may take heart and realize that your lives of love and prayer are not in vain. Indeed, they are helping to save the world and to restore it to the beauty with which its Creator endowed it."* (*The Journal of the Devotion* 302).

What does Saint Peter tell us about the worldwide Chastisement?

Like the Warning of Our Lady of Akita, Saint Peter tells us that the Chastisement will be by fire. "By the word of God heavens existed long ago, and an earth formed out of water and by means of water, through which the world that then existed was deluged with water and perished. But by the same word the heavens and earth that now exist have been stored up for fire, being kept until the day of judgment and destruction of ungodly men." (2 Peter 5-7).

Why is the worldwide Chastisement slow in coming?

Saint Peter tells us it is because the Lord is merciful and wants to bring us to repentance. Jesus King said this by quoting scripture in His urgent Warning, "Therefore you rebuke offenders little by little, warn them, and remind them of the sins they are committing, that they may abandon their wickedness and believe in you, O Lord!" (Wisdom 12:2).

Saint Peter says, "But do not ignore this one fact, beloved, that with the

Lord one day is as a thousand years, and a thousand years as one day. The Lord is not slow about his promise as some count slowness, but is forbearing toward you, not wishing that any should perish, but that all should reach repentance. But the day of the Lord will come like a thief, and then the heavens will pass away with a loud noise, and the elements will be dissolved with fire, and the earth and the works that are upon it will be burned up." (2 Peter 8-10).

How should we live as we wait for the worldwide Chastisement?

Saint Peter tells us that "since all these things are thus to be dissolved, what sort of persons ought you to be in lives of holiness and godliness, waiting for and hastening the coming of the day of God, because of which the heavens will be kindled and dissolved, and the elements will melt with fire! But according to His promise we wait for new heavens and a new earth in which righteousness dwells.

"Therefore, beloved, since you wait for these, be zealous to be found by Him without spot or blemish, and at peace. And count the forbearance of our Lord as salvation." (2 Peter 11-14).

What is a formula for protection, endurance and survival of chastisements?

God's Survival Kit: Faith in God's Protection, Prayer for Protection, Thanksgiving for Protection, Acts of Mercy for Victims and Hope for the Future.

Comments from Hurricane Charley Survivors gave us the formula above for protection, endurance and survival of chastisements.

Faith in God's Protection

"If you had faith before the hurricane, this just made it stronger," said a volunteer coordinator for an emergency relief center in Punta Gorda, Florida, the epicenter of Hurricane Charley. "If you didn't have faith, well, it probably made it worse," he added. "Some people only turn to God when they want something," said a survivor. **"But faith shouldn't be a once-in-a-while thing. We need to live it every day."**

Prayer for Protection

He and his wife recited Psalm 23 at the height of the storm, while they held pillows over their heads. They were scared, but the Psalm gave them comfort.

Another survivor recited the Rosary the night before the storm to calm her nerves. When Hurricane Charley bore down on them the next day, she and her husband, their two dogs and a neighbor squeezed into a closet in their home.

As the wind roared and chunks of their house began flying away, she shut her eyes and invoked St. Jude, the patron saint of desperate situations and hopeless causes. **"Help us survive this!"** she pleaded.

They did, and so did eight other family members who live in the area.

Thanksgiving for Protection

A minister greeted visitors to the heavily damaged sanctuary at his church. "I never saw any anger," he said. "But, I heard a lot of **'Thank you, Lord, for a new day to serve you.'** "

Acts of Mercy for the Victims

A survivor directed the flow of cars into his church's parking lot for a week. They unloaded cartons of food, water and ice dropped off by strangers, and helped victims choose badly needed items to get them through the crisis. He gave hugs, offered prayers and handed bottles of cold water to motorists stuck in traffic jams on the adjoining street.

His house escaped damage. The way he saw it, if God spared him, it's his responsibility to heed Jesus who said, **"Whatever you do for the least of these, you do for me."** "I know how blessed I am," he said, "so I want to give back."

Husband and wife survivors, who own a contracting business, gave temporary work to local Mexicans left jobless by the closures of so many area restaurants.

"Give me one can of spaghetti sauce and I'll feed 50," said another survivor. He and his wife suffered storm damage, but they knew pretty much everyone else did as well. So, he volunteered to cook meals for the hungry on a propane camp stove in their church kitchen. "Right now, there are so many holes in the dikes, and just so many fingers to plug them," he said. **"But God hasn't abandoned us. If anything, this will give us a chance to see His grace more clearly in our lives."**

Hope for the Future

A victim of the hurricane said, "We're looking at this as God giving us a new direction in life." She donated the inventory salvaged from their destroyed bakery business to a local church. As soon as they pick up the salvage of their lives, she and her husband will go on with hope in some new business. "We got a message and we intend to listen to it," she said.

A survivor understood why some homeless victims were angry, frustrated and without hope. But, for those who told him so, he had a ready answer. "I told them that there's a force stronger than Hurricane Charley that can change their life for the positive," he says. It's hope!

"We feel blessed and absolutely grateful," another survivor said. **"Every day we wake up is a good one, even if things are a little difficult right now. Life is beautiful."**

Why do we face so much evil?

Pope John Paul II said, "In the face of the evil that manifests itself in different ways in the world, man, afflicted and disconcerted, asks: 'Why?' "
He continued,

> At this dawn of the third millennium, blessed by the Great Jubilee and rich in potential, humanity is marked by the distressing spread of terrorism. The succession of atrocious attacks on human life perturbs and disquiets consciences and arouses in believers the deeply felt question that recurs in the Psalms: "Why, Lord? How long?"
>
> God has responded to this anguished question that arises from the scandal of evil, not with an explanation of principle, as though wishing to justify Himself, but with the sacrifice of His own Son on the Cross. In Jesus' death are found the apparent triumph of evil and the definitive victory of good; the darkest moment of history and the revelation of divine glory; the breaking point is the center of attraction and reconstruction of the universe. "I," Jesus says, "when I am lifted up from the earth, will draw all men to myself." (John 12:32). The Cross of Christ is, for believers, [an] icon of hope because on it was accomplished the salvific plan of the love of God. . . .
>
> With our gaze fixed on Christ crucified, in spiritual union with the Virgin Mary, let us continue on our way, sustained by the power of the Resurrection.
> (Pope John Paul II, Angelus Address, September 19, 2004).

Appendix
Prayers of the Devotion

The Novena in Honor of Jesus as True King

This simple Novena is a most generous gift from Our Lord. Jesus gave these extraordinary promises: *"I promise you that every time you say these Novena prayers I will convert ten sinners, bring ten souls into the One True Faith, release ten souls from Purgatory, many of whom are the souls of priests, and* **be less severe in My judgment of your nation.***"*

The Novena consists of praying once a day over a period of nine days a set of one OUR FATHER, one HAIL MARY and one GLORY BE, recited along with the following Novena Prayer:

O Lord our God, You alone are the Most Holy King and Ruler of all nations. We pray to You, Lord, in the great expectation of receiving from You, O Divine King, mercy, peace, justice and all good things.

Protect, O Lord our King, our families and the land of our birth. Guard us, we pray, Most Faithful One! Protect us from our enemies and from Your Just Judgment.

Forgive us, O Sovereign King, our sins against You. Jesus, You are King of Mercy. We have deserved Your Just Judgment. Have mercy on us, Lord, and forgive us. We trust in Your Great Mercy.

O most awe-inspiring King, we bow before You and pray; may Your Reign, Your Kingdom, be recognized on earth! Amen.

Jesus said, *"I desire that this Novena be prayed on the nine days preceding My Feast of Christ the King, but I encourage souls to pray this Novena at any time throughout the year. My promises will be granted whenever it is prayed."*

Novena of Holy Communions

This Novena consists of offering nine consecutive Holy Communions in honor of Jesus King of All Nations. Jesus said, *"I desire that the faithful souls who embrace this devotion to Me. . . .make a Novena of Holy Communions. They therefore shall offer me nine (9) consecutive Holy Communions, and go to Confession during this Novena, if possible, in honor of Me as 'Jesus King of All Nations.' "*

Jesus indicated that by "consecutive," He meant nine Communions, uninterrupted, one after another, that the soul would receive. They need not be on nine calendar days in a row, just each Communion received, one after the other.

The powerful and unprecedented effects of this Novena were shown to Jesus' "servant" in a vision. She saw Jesus gazing up to Heaven. Nine times He gave a command and an angel came to earth. Jesus explained, *"My daughter, for those souls who will offer Me [this] devotion I will bid an angel of each of the Nine Choirs, one with each Holy Communion, to guard this soul for the rest of its life on this earth."*

Jesus wants us to pray the Novena for others, and explains its necessity at this time. *"This Novena may be prayed with its promises for another soul, and that soul will also receive additional angelic protection. I urge My faithful ones to offer Me this Novena again and again so that I may continue to send down My holy angels for the protection and assistance of other souls who cannot do this for themselves. In these end-times the power of the enemy has greatly increased. I see how greatly My children are in need of My protection."*

In His great generosity, Jesus granted that, in addition to the angelic protection, one may have a separate, unrelated intention for this Novena. He promised, *"What they ask for in this Novena, if it be according to My Most Holy Will, I will surely grant it. Let these souls ask from Me without reservation."*

Consecration to Mary Mediatrix of All Grace

Jesus asks those who embrace this devotion to consecrate themselves to His mother under her title as "Mary, Mediatrix of All Grace." His servant recorded Jesus' words.

"My beloved little daughter, your Lord and God comes to you to give you a message of great importance. I desire that the souls who embrace My devotion to 'Jesus King of All Nations,' make a special consecration to My Most Holy Mother under her title of 'Mary Mediatrix of All Grace,' which it has pleased Me in My Great Love for her to give her. People MUST acknowledge her indispensable role as the Mediatrix, the Channel, of all of My Graces to mankind. Only when this dogma is officially proclaimed by My Church will I truly establish My Reign on earth."

Our Lady then appeared next to Our Lord and said: "Daughter, know that I have obtained this prayer for my children from the Heart of my Divine Son."

Jesus then revealed the Prayer of Consecration to Mary, Mediatrix of All Grace:

O Mary, Most Holy and Immaculate Mother of God, of Jesus, our Victim-High Priest, True Prophet, and Sovereign King, I come to you as the Mediatrix of All Grace, for that is truly what you are. O Fountain of all Grace! O Fairest of Roses! Most Pure Spring! Unsullied Channel of all God's grace! Receive me, Most Holy Mother! Present me and my every need to the Most Holy Trinity! That having been made pure and holy in His Sight through your hands, they may return to me, through you, as graces and blessings. I give and consecrate myself to you, Mary, Mediatrix of All Grace, that Jesus, Our One True Mediator, Who is the King of All Nations, may Reign in every heart. Amen.

Jesus also gave this beautiful message:

"My Children, I desire only your peace and happiness! My Most Holy Mother has appealed to you time and time again! She still pleads. . . . Children, <u>listen</u> to your Heavenly Mother. Is there a more tender or loving ambassadress than My own Mother? You see, My children, if I had come to you in My Power and Majesty before this, before My Most Holy Mother had come to you in great tenderness and meekness, you would not have been able to handle it for fear. The times have arrived, My children. Your Lord comes to you with great Power and Majesty. My Most Holy Mother has prepared My Way, with the greatest of care. My children, you owe much, very much, to your Heavenly Mother."

On December 12, 1993, the Feast of Our Lady of Guadalupe, Our Lord Jesus Christ spoke the following about His Mother,

"Mary never Reigns more Queenly than when She Loves most Motherly." He said, "Make this known."

The Chaplet of Unity

The Chaplet of Unity is a series of prayers recited on ordinary Rosary beads. Jesus said, *"I promise to give this Chaplet of Unity great power over My Wounded Sacred Heart when prayed with faith and confidence to heal the brokenness of My peoples' lives. . . ."*

Recite on the large bead before each of the five decades:

God Our Heavenly Father, through Your Son Jesus, our Victim-High Priest, True Prophet and Sovereign King, pour forth the power of Your Holy Spirit upon us and open our hearts. In Your great mercy, through the Motherly mediation of the Blessed Virgin Mary, Our Queen, forgive our sinfulness, heal our brokenness and renew our hearts in the faith and peace and love and joy of Your Kingdom, that we may be one in You.

Recite on the ten small beads of each of the five decades:

In Your great mercy, forgive our sinfulness, heal our brokenness and renew our hearts, that we may be one in You.

Conclude the Chaplet with the following prayers:

Hear, O Israel! The Lord our God is One God!
O Jesus, King of All Nations, may Your Reign be recognized on earth!
Mary, Our Mother and Mediatrix of All Grace, pray and intercede for us your children!
St. Michael, Great Prince and Guardian of your people, come with the Holy Angels and Saints and protect us! Amen.

Jesus said, *"Yes, in this devotion to Me as Jesus, King of All Nations, entreat My Kingly Heart with the prayer of this Chaplet of Unity that I Myself, Your Sovereign Lord Jesus Christ, have given you! Pray and ask for the spiritual wholeness and the healing of your own souls, for the union of your own will with God's Will, for the healing of your families, friends, enemies, relationships, religious orders, communities, countries, nations, the world, and unity within My Church under the Holy Father! I shall grant many spiritual, physical, emotional and psychological healings for those who pray this prayer if it is beneficial to their salvation according to My Holy Will! Unity and oneness in Spirit was My Own prayer for all mankind and My Church as My own last testament before I gave My life as Savior of all mankind! As I am One with My Father and the Holy Spirit, My Will is that all mankind be one in Me, so that one Faith, one Fold, and one Shepherd will be gathered together under My Sovereign Kingship as Lord."*

"I, Jesus, Son of the Most High God . . . promise to hold our to the souls who pray My Chaplet of Unity the Sceptor of My Kingship and grant them mercy, pardon and protection in times of severe weather and plagues. I extend this promise not only for yourselves, but also for individuals for whom you pray. Any harm or danger, spiritual or physical, whether it be to soul, mind or body, will I protect these souls against, and clothe them over with My Own mantle of Kingly Mercy."

The Chaplet of Unity may also be prayed as a novena, nine times in succession. This can be done at one time, hourly or daily. Jesus said, *"Make a Novena to Me of the Chaplet of Unity and I will powerfully and expediently answer your prayers according to My Sovereign and Most Holy Will!"*

Dan Lynch Productions

Our Lady of Guadalupe, Hope for the World

" This **book** will instruct, encourage and inspire a wide variety of people in the Church and outside the Church."

Fr. Frank Pavone, National Director Priests for Life

Teresita's Choices

If you want to know the truth about the consequences of real choices for pre-marital sex and abortion, you should read this **book**!

If you want to know the truth about the consequences of respect for life and the dignity of all human beings of all races from conception until natural death, you should read this book.

Our Lady of Guadalupe, Mother of Hope!

In this **video**, see and hear from Guadalupe experts and the Pope in Mexico with the Mother of Hope.

Reviews by producers Ted Flynn, Tom Petrisko, Drew Mariani and Ignatius Press say: "Stirring, gripping, comprehensive with moving testimonies!"

How to Be Holy

Pope John Paul II inaugurated the Third Millennium by consecrating it to Our Lady. This is a set of four **audio** tapes or three CDs of a retreat on the Holy Father's plan for the Third Millennium. It consists of four talks: Personal Holiness, Knowing God, Loving God and Serving God.

Order Form
Dan Lynch Productions

Teresita's Choices	Book	$12.95	_____
Our Lady of Guadalupe, Hope for the World	Book	$14.95	_____
Our Lady of Guadalupe, Mother of Hope Please specify English or Spanish	VHS DVD	$19.95 $23.95	_____ _____
How to Be Holy	Audio CD	$14.95 $22.95	_____ _____
The Call to Total Consecration to the Immaculate Heart of Mary	Book	$ 9.95	_____
Prayers for Peace	Booklet	$ 3.95	_____
Prayers for Life	Booklet	$ 3.95	_____
St. Therese - A Guide to Her Life and Her Movie	Booklet	$ 4.95	_____
Chastisements - How to Prepare and Pray Against Them	Booklet	$ 4.95	_____
The Way of the Cross with Our Lady of Guadalupe	Booklet	$ 5.95	_____

SHIPPING & HANDLING
UNITED STATES

Value of Order	S & H
$ 0.00 - $ 9.99	$5.00
$ 10.00 - $24.99	$6.00
$ 25.00 - $49.99	$7.00
$ 50.00 - $99.99	$8.00
$100.00 & up	10% of order

-CANADIAN-
Double Above Rates
-FOREIGN-
Triple Above Rates

Subtotal $_____

Shipping & Handling $_____
(Must be included with all orders)

Optional Donation $_____

Total Due $_____

Method of Payment to JKMI Press:

Check Enclosed   Money Order   VISA   MasterCard   Discover

Credit Card Account Number   Expiration Date (MM/YY)

Name & Signature as it appears on card: _____

Name _____

Address _____

City / State / Zip _____

Daytime Phone(____) _____ E-mail _____

JKMI Press 144 Sheldon Road St. Albans, VT 05478
Phone - 888-834-6261 WebSite - www.JKMIPress.com